Fight With Me

Dear Charlotte & Philip,
Hope you enjoy the book!
Your friend Oliver

Fight With Me

How We Learned to be Married

TIM AND OLIVE CHAN

ISBN: 0-9918109-5-3
ISBN-13: 978-0-9918109-5-6

Cover design by Bill Vaxevanis
Cover illustration by Olive Chan
Interior design and typesetting by Tim Chan

This book is dedicated to our parents:
Louis and Janice,
Ben and Bernadette.

Thank you for loving us,
for showing us
the joys and struggles of marriage,
and for living out your love.

Contents

Adjusting the Well-Oiled Machine

My Burnout Experience (Olive's story)

How My Husband Helped Me Most

The Challenge of Having a Burnt Out Wife

Looking Out for Her Best Interest

Facing Depression (Tim's story)

Wait with Me

Limping Along with My Husband

Seeing Beyond the Darkness

The "N" Word

You're Not the Same Person I Married!

A Daily Connection Point

The Fun Factor

Taking It Into the Bedroom

When I Don't Feel the Love

Love that Lasts a Lifetime

Foreword

This is not a "how to" book on marriage. It is more of a "how we" book. We won't tell you how to build your marriage, but we will share with you how we bumbled along and tried to make the most of our first few years of marriage.

We are by no means experts and our experience is guaranteed to be different from yours, but we share our story on the off chance that you might benefit from what we learned the hard way (or at least be somewhat entertained). Having freshly come out of the initial childless season of our marriage, some of our experiences may seem immature or unpolished. This is not an oversight. We want to capture these memories now before they fade over time. While we cannot claim to offer you answers for your relationship, our hope in the writing of this book is that you, our reader, would find in us a friendly voice to accompany you on your journey forward.

Thank you for reading our book! This is the first book that we have written together. Though much of what we say is with one voice, we each wrote different parts of the book from our own unique perspectives. Most chapters are written from one of our perspectives (with the exception of Chapter 6 where we alternate). We are extremely grateful for the encouragement, comments, support, and feedback we've received from our readers along the way and look forward to hearing your response to this book.

Special thanks to our family: Ben, Bernadette, Louis, Janice, Dan, Tiff, Simon, and Alena for their love and for believing in us. Thanks to Melissa Foo, Carrie Zubik, Amelia Rana, Lucas Lee, Cam Ludwig, Paul Sohn, and Mike Poon for reading our crappy drafts and sparing others from having to wade through incomplete thoughts and run-on sentences. Any mistakes that remain are solely our fault. Thanks to Bill Vaxevanis, for his excellent design work on our book cover. Thanks to Neal and June Black for sharing their wisdom during our engagement and in our first few years of marriage. Thanks to God for giving us this season of life to write this book.

Introduction

Life as we knew it was about to end. I was notified of this change at 3 a.m. on a Monday morning.

"Are you awake?" a voice that sounded like my wife's whispered to me in the dark.

"Maybe," I mumbled.

"You're going to be a dad," said Olive.

It took a while to sink in; partly because it was such big news and partly because it was the middle of the night. Seriously, who delivers news like this at 3 a.m. in the morning?? I believe my response was, "How do YOU know?"

There is a phrase in Chinese that refers to a "two person paradise." Some days I could use this phrase to describe our marriage. Though our first few years had its fair share of difficulties, they were very enjoyable. But even in the midst of the joy of anticipating first-time parenthood there was a hint of sadness, knowing that the sweetness of the initial season of our marriage was coming to an end.

Olive and I met as university students on a trip to Japan. She made quite the impression on me. She was beautiful, talented, fun, and laughed at my jokes. During that trip, we developed a friendship that we were able to maintain while she lived in the East and Far East (Toronto and Asia) and I in the West (Vancouver). Three years later we started dating long-distance. 17 months after that we were engaged.

Our wedding was held on a beautiful, sunny day in Toronto over the Thanksgiving weekend. Two days later, we celebrated with our family and friends on a cold and rainy day in Vancouver, which is where we ended up settling.

After two weeks of honeymooning in Oregon, we returned to begin our real life as a married couple. We didn't quite know what to expect. What we did know was that our first years of marriage were a critical time to set a foundation for our entire future together. We could only go through it once, so we might as well try to make it count as much as possible.

Little did we expect the dark days ahead as one of us walked the road of recovery from burnout and the other would struggle with depression. Neither of us anticipated the rich lessons that marriage taught us about how to live and how to love.

"Life can only be understood backward; but it must be lived forwards," Soren Kierkegaard observed. As Olive and I have paused to reflect on our first years of marriage, we have seen things that we could only understand in retrospect.

This is the story of how we learned to be married.

CHAPTER ONE

With This Boxing Glove, I Thee Wed

◆ CONFLICT ◆

Learning to Fight

There's one thing I regret about my marriage. I regret not fighting with my wife more.

It seems like a strange thing to regret. Isn't fighting bad in a marriage? Shouldn't we be avoiding it? Isn't the picture of a great marriage a husband and wife who get along well and don't fight? No. We believe fighting is an important part of a healthy marriage.

By "fight" I mean the conflict, argument, or conversation that results from a disagreement. How we fight might be different from how you fight. We know friends who are passionate people, whose fighting involves shouting, some pushing, and the occasional teddy bear thrown across the room. For us, since we are more laid-back (and lazy), our fighting looks like a regular conversation with a few more frowns and eye-rolls (and tears for one of us, although I won't say who).

Olive and I both grew up avoiding fights with people. We'd rather hide what we truly felt than have to face the awkwardness and pain of conflict. When we got married we first had to learn to fight. Then we had to learn how to resolve the fight.

My Odd Engagement Gift to My Wife

When I proposed to Olive I gave her several gifts. One of the gifts was a pair of boxing gloves. When she opened the gift, she was surprised. Attached was a note that said, "Our relationship has had its share of fights, challenges, and difficulties. We have and are continuing to learn how to work through these. The boxing gloves are for us to share. One for you, one for me. We will fight together. Will you fight with me?"

What I wanted us to remember was this: When we are fighting with each other, we are not fighting against each other.

Though at the moment we may be angry and fighting with each other, in the bigger picture, both of us are on the same team. Together, we are working to build a healthy marriage by resolving the conflict in our relationship. When we are fighting with each other, we are not trying to win as individuals but we're trying to win as a team.

The Fight We Never Had (But I Wish We Did)

I wish we had this fight a long time ago. But as I write, we've managed to avoid fighting about this issue… for almost four years.

It's about vitamins.

Olive grew up in a family that took vitamins, fish oils, iron, probiotics, beeswax, organic worm chest hairs, and a plethora of health products. I hardly took any vitamins growing up (though my parents tried to encourage me). When we moved in together, Olive brought her bottles and bottles of vitamins with her.

Then I started seeing the bills for the vitamins. My eyes popped out! We quickly had a discussion about it. When I told Olive how much her vitamins cost, even she was surprised. It was something her parents had paid for. She never really looked at the cost.

Here was the issue: Olive was convinced of the value of the vitamins she was taking while I did not see the value. But we were very early into our marriage and we both didn't want to make a big deal out of it. Looking back now, we were still uneasy about having conflict and fighting, so we avoided it as much as possible. We sidestepped the fight and quickly ended up compromising. She would do with fewer vitamins, and I would let her continue buying them.

"Phew!" we thought. "Mission accomplished. Conflict avoided. That's good right?"

Not really.

To this day, every time I see the vitamins I cringe. I think they are a waste of money. I actually feel a bit of resentment towards Olive because I'm not happy with the decision we made.

She probably doesn't know that this bothers me still. How could she? I've kept silent all this time and kept it inside. (As I write this chapter, I am slowly convincing myself that we need to have this fight. I guess this is my way of indirectly trying to instigate the fight. Maybe when she reads the draft on this chapter, then she'll know and we'll finally end up having the fight.)

This is why it's important for us to have fights and then to resolve the conflict. If conflict is not resolved, the resentment builds up over time and gradually pulls the couple apart. It might seem like something small (like vitamins), but underneath there are larger issues. Untreated, those issues accumulate over time and grow into serious problems.

Woodpeckers and Turtles

A couple we respect greatly and who do premarital counseling with many couples (including us) gave us this extremely helpful illustration. When it comes to conflict resolution, most people fall into one of two camps: Turtles or Woodpeckers.

Turtles are those who resist addressing the issue and shy away from talking about what's upsetting them. Fighting seems like a dangerous activity and they could get hurt, so they hide away in their shell. When it comes to fighting, turtles need to learn to take a risk, stick their heads out of their shells and engage.

Woodpeckers are the opposite. They want to talk about conflict right away and they will be very vocal about what's bothering them. They never shy away from a fight and if they're dealing with a turtle, they'll peck and peck with their questions and comments to try to get the other person to talk.

Woodpeckers need to learn to tone it down, listen and give the other person space to speak.

Olive and I are both turtle types. It means that we have had to be very intentional about mustering up the courage to say what's on our minds. We've found that with each fight and conversation we've had, it has built our sense of safety for the next time around. Because both of us would rather avoid conflict, what we've really had to work on is initiating the fight.

The Time I Made the Bride and Groom Fight

This past summer I was invited to give the homily at my friends' wedding. Do you ever remember the homily at a wedding? I usually don't. I wanted to spare the couple (and all their family and friends) of a boring speech. So I tried to make the homily memorable.

During my talk, I presented them with a gift: A pair of boxing gloves, one for each of them. Then I taught them how to fight fairly using a technique called reflective listening. This is what I said:

"Each person has to have the chance to talk while the other listens. The person who listens must listen without interrupting, without explaining, without being defensive. Their only job is to listen and understand – to make sure they've heard the other person correctly.

Then you switch and it's the other person's turn to talk.

Each person must have the opportunity to share his or her point of view with the other. Each must have the opportunity to reflect back the other person's point of view. And most importantly, each person must be reassured that the other person has understood them.

That's a fair fight.

Why do you want to fight well? According to marriage authors Drs. Les and Leslie Parrott, 90% of fights are resolved if you can empathize with the other person[1]. One of the main reasons for arguments and conflicts in a marriage is misunderstanding and miscommunication. When we are able to understand the other person's point of view, most of the conflicts are resolved."

I asked them to put on their boxing glove and start fighting – in the middle of their wedding ceremony, with all their family and friends as witnesses.

For the first round, I got the bride to do the punching (talking), while the groom would block (listening and understanding) without throwing any punches back. During the second round, the groom would punch and the bride would block.

They fought each other that day. I don't think the couple will ever forget their wedding homily.

Choosing a Suitable Time and Location to Talk

Many people live by the advice "don't go to bed angry." Some people take this literally in their marriage, and make it a point to resolve their conflict before the day is over. For us, we've found that taking this advice literally has not always worked well. Instead, we understand "don't go to bed angry" as not to put off fighting and resolving conflict – to address it as soon as we can.

Olive is usually quite tired and an emotional eggshell by the end of the day. She is also pretty groggy first thing in the morning. I'm not very good at multi-tasking – so it's hard for me to drive and have deep conversation at the same time.

We've learned that those times are not good times for us to try to resolve conflict. We've learned to say, "I've been feeling upset about [fill in the blank], can we talk about it [suggest a time]?"

Working through conflict requires energy and full attention. We want to set ourselves up for success in choosing a time and place where we can talk without interruptions, distractions or needing to feel rushed. Sometimes, it means scheduling it for the next day or in a couple days, even. Another advantage of setting aside time to talk is that it gives both of us some space to process what happened so that we don't come flying at each other with emotionally charged accusations.

The time in between scheduling the fight and actually having the fight feels awkward. During that time, I am always a bit anxious about how the fight will go and if we will end up resolving it well. That's why we make it a priority to have the conversation as soon as appropriate.

The Role of a Trusted Friend

In the rare case when I am especially upset at my wife or particularly confused at what is going on, I find it helpful to speak to a trusted friend before the fight. When I speak to a friend, I am looking for a chance to be heard and understood – someone to tell me that I am not crazy, or that I'm being unreasonable.

I give permission to my friend to tell it like it is, and he has to have the courage to confront me when I am wrong without being afraid that I will get angry or that it will jeopardize the friendship. Speaking to a friend is especially helpful for me as I am a verbal processor. Having the conversation often helps me to work through my emotions. On the odd occasion, I am looking for advice. And a good friend knows when to just listen and when to speak.

Though it feels strange for Olive to know that I am talking to someone else about her, she knows that I am speaking to a friend who is trustworthy and will not share our conversation with anyone. She also trusts that I will not say anything that will damage her reputation or our relationship.

For Olive, because she is an internal processor, she finds journaling as a helpful activity to help her sort out what she is feeling and thinking. Often before we have a fight, she will take time by herself to journal.

Articulating Apologies and Forgiveness

At the end of a good fight, after each person has had a chance to speak and has felt heard, apologies and forgiveness bring closure to that particular incident. The practice of saying "I'm sorry for…" and "I forgive you for…" serve to cement and affirm the relationship.

At first, when Olive would apologize to me, my response would be, "It's okay." But after reflecting on this, I realized that I didn't really mean what I was saying. I was lying. It wasn't okay – I was hurt. Saying, "It's okay" seemed to minimize what had just happened. In a way, it was a form of pride. I was pretending that I was strong and that I couldn't be hurt.

What I've learned to do instead of responding with "It's okay," is to say, "I forgive you for…" As much humility and courage as it takes to ask for forgiveness, it also requires an amount of humility and courage to offer forgiveness. It takes humility to acknowledge your hurt to your spouse and courage to let go of the hurt.

Resolving the Vitamin Fight

Shortly after I wrote the draft of this chapter, Olive walked into the room and started flipping through a magazine.

"So, I read the draft of your chapter," she said.

"Oh," I replied slowly. At this moment, I thought about what she just said and what it meant. It seemed as if both of us turtles were mustering up the courage to poke out our heads and start a fight.

"So, what did you think?" I finally blurted, after an awkward amount of silence.

"It was good. I liked it." There was more silence. Then I laughed a little. It was one of those fake laughs that I sometimes give when I'm nervous about something.

"We should probably talk about the vitamins," Olive said.

"Yes, we should," I replied feeling relieved that she had finally brought up subject.

"When?" she asked.

"Good question… how about tonight?"

"Tonight?" Olive asked, a bit surprised at how soon it would be.

"We can have our fight after the baby sleeps. I guess we'd better not procrastinate… like I wrote about in the chapter."

"Okay, then it's a date."

"A fight date!" I said with a smile.

It's easy for me to tell when conflict is not fully resolved. When I think of an incident and I feel regret, guilt, anger, or resentment, I know something is wrong. My tendency to avoid the conflict and bury the feelings is only a temporary solution. Sooner or later those feelings creep up again. I was glad we were going to fight. Unresolved conflict was tiring.

That night, after we put our baby to sleep, we both settled comfortably on the couch and started fighting. I started first, sharing my perspective and how I felt. Olive confirmed that she understood what I was saying. Then Olive shared how she felt, and I reflected back to her what I had understood. As we talked and listened, it became clear to us what the fight was really about.

The root issue for me was my concern about our finances and how much we were spending on vitamins (and on everything else as well). We had just decided to be writers and would not have much income in the near future. For Olive, it was a concern for her health and well-being, and how vitamins contributed to that. In fact, finances and Olive's health were things that both of us were concerned about. This realization affirmed that we were on the same team.

Then we started exploring possible solutions with the confidence that we were on the same page. After some research, we decided to try out a solution, and re-evaluate in a few months to see how it was going.

The fight took all evening. We were exhausted afterwards and ready to sleep. Perhaps there were faster ways to do this. But this was what worked for us.

I'm glad that we took the time in our first years of marriage to figure out this fighting and resolving business. With each new fight, it takes a little less time and a little less energy. It also feels less risky. We have an idea what to expect and how to prepare. And we know that if we take the time and effort to fight fairly, we will be able to resolve the conflict and continue to deepen our marriage. After years of figuring out how to fight with each other, we are more comfortable with saying, "Fight with *me*," because we know that by saying so we also mean, "Fight *with* me."

When I was thinking about writing this chapter, I reminisced with Olive about the fights that we have had. Because we had forgiven each other, we were free to talk about those incidents openly.

CHAPTER TWO

The Invention of Blue Days

◆ VISION ◆

How Marriage is Like Painting

The summer before our daughter was born, Olive and I had a chance to work on a painting together. It was the first time we had done this. We had visited Whiffen Spit near Victoria, BC and were captivated with its breathtaking view. Inspired by what we saw, we bought a large, 3 feet by 4 feet canvas and set to work.

Painting together was very different from painting alone. We weren't sure what to do at first or how to start. So we talked about the process, brainstormed some ideas, and tried a few things out. Some parts of the painting we worked on together at the same time, while other parts we worked on individually. Every now and then we would check in with each other to make sure things fit together and decide on what to do next.

The process of turning an empty white canvas into a piece of beautiful art was challenging and enjoyable. At times I would sit back and watch Olive's talent at work. At times Olive would stop and watch me work. Sometimes I felt frustrated at the part I was working on and was glad to have Olive there to help me. My favourite moments were when we were finished painting for the day and paused to admire what we had achieved.

After a week of working together, the painting was finished. We felt an immense amount of satisfaction and pride having completed the work of art together as a team. It turned out better than either of us had expected.

In a way, our lives are like a large canvas, and our decisions and actions are like paint. When we decided to get married, it was like we were saying, "Instead of painting individually, let's paint together. Let's merge our efforts and work on this canvas of life together."

How Blue Days Came to Be

Living life with Olive inspires me. Her vision of life is distinct from mine. What she sees and hopes for challenges me. It gives me different perspective and fresh ideas. I think that's one of the things I appreciate about having a wife.

When I was single, I had an idea of what I wanted my life

to look like. Olive also had her own idea of what she wanted her life to look like. When we got married, we quickly realized the need to develop a combined vision for the future. Sometimes our ideas clashed and one idea would win out over the other. Other times, those ideas fused together and something completely new would emerge.

The amalgamation of our ideas didn't happen naturally. Much of it was intentional. It required the sharing of our ideas, the willingness to be vulnerable about our hopes and fears, the letting go of our past traditions, and the desire to forge a new path on our journey forward.

While a handful of these deeper conversations happened in day-to-day life, we noticed that most of our usual conversations were more superficial in nature. Our everyday conversations were about things like, "Should we buy butter or margarine?" or "Where do you want to go on vacation?" The larger and more significant questions such as, "What value will family have in our lives?" and "Which people and activities do we want to shape us?" rarely came up. To remedy this, we invented "Blue Days."

During the first three years of our marriage, we dedicated an entire day each quarter of the year to talk about our lives and future. These were our Blue Days.

Why blue?

In the Birkman Method® personality test[2], the colour blue is used to describe a person's strength in creativity, design, thought, and planning. These are strengths in both Olive's and my Birkman tests. We love thinking, creating, and designing; and this is the essence of Blue Days.

During our Blue Days, we would reflect on the important parts of our lives and evaluate how things were going in these areas. We dreamed about how we hoped these areas would look like in the future and decided on what things we wanted to change.

Why Reflection is Important to Us

"Busy" is a word many people use to describe their life. Their life is full. There are many things to do. Life is constantly go-go-go. Our lives used to be like that. Describing my life as being busy made me feel important, needed, and significant. I liked those feelings. We both lived this way until we discovered the value of stopping to reflect.

Reflection reminds me to be grateful. When I take time to consider how blessed I am in many areas of my life, I feel gratitude. Gratitude gives me perspective and helps to counter the complaining and negativity that so easily creep into my life.

Reflection allows me to evaluate the direction of my life. When I spend my days crammed with going from one thing to the next, it is hard to see what is really going on. When I take the time to step back from the day-to-day busyness of life, I am able to see the bigger picture.

Reflection gives me time to decide what the important things in my life will be and what my life will be about.

When practiced as a couple, reflecting allows us to evaluate and adjust our direction in life. As we reflect, we have the time and space we need to make difficult decisions. It also gives us the opportunity to make sure that how we spend our time, energy, and money align with what our beliefs and values are. It allows us to be intentional.

Why Dreaming is Important to Us

Ordinary living can get tiring. The humdrum of working, cooking meals, the never-ending pile of dishes to wash, the loads of laundry, the bills to pay, the emails to return… all of it can weigh us down. Our Blue Days have allowed us to step away from the endless chores of life to take a breath and dream together.

During the months before our daughter was born, we felt so burdened by everything we had to do. There was a car seat to find, baby stuff to pick up from relatives, the nursery to prepare, prenatal classes to attend, a name to choose, and the list went on and on. Two months before the due date, we had a chance to get away for a day. We talked about what we hoped our family would be like. We dreamed about how we wanted our daughter to experience love in her family, how we wanted her to grow up knowing that she was valued apart from her accomplishments, and how we hoped to help her discover her gifts and talents. This dreaming got us excited and gave us the strength to continue with the hard work of preparing for the baby's arrival.

When we remind ourselves of our vision of the future, we gain passion for where we are heading and what's to come. It renews our energy to continue with the routines of each day, knowing that we are moving toward our dreams.

A Typical Blue Day

Our Blue Days generally took place in January, April, July, and October. October was when we celebrated our wedding anniversary; so every year we took a short trip to celebrate.

One of those days was designated a Blue Day.

We tried several different venues for our Blue Days. Initially, we would book a local bed and breakfast, check in and talk during the evening and the next morning. This didn't work that well because we had to check in after 4 p.m. and check out by 11 a.m. the next day. It didn't give us enough time to talk. We tried staying at home for our Blue Day. The advantages of this were saving on cost and travel time and being able to sleep in our own bed. But we had to be very disciplined to stay focused because things around the house easily distracted us. What worked well was finding someplace quiet we could go to for the day. Once, we borrowed my brother's apartment while he was at work. We also tried using an extra room in our friends' basement. Another time we booked a room at a local bed & breakfast from ten in the morning until five in the afternoon. These all worked well for us as we ended up having the privacy we needed and a pleasant and comfortable venue to think and talk.

In the weeks and days leading up to a Blue Day, we would prepare by noting down topics and issues we wanted to discuss. The night before our Blue Day, we would make sure to sleep a bit earlier so what we would be alert and awake to talk the next day.

The first thing we did after breakfast was take some time to reflect and journal on our own. Then we would get together and start going over the important areas of our lives. We'd make sure our cell phones were turned off and only used the laptop when we needed to. We took notes on sheets of different coloured paper to make things a bit more fun, and wrote down any action points we wanted to implement after the day was over.

The Ten Important Parts of Our Lives

Over the course of each Blue Day we would talk about ten important parts of our lives. We would spend about 20-40 minutes on each topic, depending on whether there was a lot to decide on or not. We'd always begin with The Big Picture, and we'd usually end with Finances, but aside from that, we talked about whatever we felt like talking about next.

Here are the topics (see the Appendix for a description of each topic and a list of questions that guided our conversations):

- The Big Picture
- Marriage
- Family
- Friends
- Faith Community
- Work
- Rest
- Growth and Health
- Life Infrastructure
- Finances

We kept all our notes in one folder and every time we had a Blue Day, we brought the folder with us. We briefly reviewed the notes we took from last time and added to them accordingly. Over time, we could look back and see how we'd grown and changed, as well as see which things had slipped through the cracks.

The Blue Days in our first three years of marriage really helped solidify our marriage. Our discussions were helpful in getting us on the same page and understanding each other.

Ultimately, they gave us the time and space to make our own decisions as a couple that would end up shaping our future.

CHAPTER THREE

If You Could Read My Mind

◆ COMMUNICATION ◆

What I Say Isn't Always What I Mean

"So, what kind of jam would you like me to pick up?" asked Tim as we drove to the grocery store.

"Oh, whatever. It doesn't matter," I replied nonchalantly.

"Strawberry?"

"No."

"Blueberry?"

"Um, I don't really like blueberry jam."

"Grape?"

I shook my head, "Nah."

"So….???"

"Just get the kind we always get. Peach!" I exclaimed.

We looked at each other and laughed.

Then, I sheepishly added, "I guess I didn't mean it when I said it didn't matter."

Something we learned early on in our relationship was that communicating well took time and effort. At times, it was due to what we said or heard. Maybe one of us would say something we didn't really mean. Maybe the other person heard wrongly or we just weren't getting each other. Other times, it was because of how we communicated.

Tim and I were both indirect communicators, but between the two of us, I was more indirect than he was. Sometimes I felt bad for him because it was as if I expected him to read my mind. I had to practice saying what I actually meant instead of hinting at it or approaching it in a roundabout way.

Are You Even Paying Attention?

Aside from learning to say what we meant, part of communicating well also included learning to observe whether or not the other person had heard us rightly. When we were first married, we would often have conversations that went something along these lines:

"Tim, can you please [fill in the blank]?"

"Mmhmm," he would reply.

"Thanks!"

Time would pass.

"Tim, I thought I asked you to [fill in the blank]?"

"You did?" he would ask, sounding genuinely surprised.

"?!?!"

From these conversations, I learned two things: 1) Tim was a terrible multitasker. 2) Just because Tim uttered a response, it didn't mean he consciously registered the thought. Part of my learning to communicate with Tim was to gauge whether he was in the frame of mind to hear what I had to say. If he was occupied with something else, I had to hold the thought and wait until he looked at me and acknowledged our interaction. To be honest, sometimes waiting to talk took a lot of discipline on my part.

Shooting Myself In the Foot

Another lesson I learned was if I wanted to initiate a conversation, I needed to make sure I was not distracted either.

There were times when I would catch myself asking Tim a question while I was doing the dishes and then miss his answer because I turned on the faucet right after I asked the question. It was a terrible habit that was unfair to Tim and frustrating for me. Again, I had to hold my thought until I could pay full attention to his answers.

Why Do We Want to Communicate Well?

A wise couple once gave us this piece of advice: "You can get really good at communicating with each other, but if you aren't friends, you'll just be really good at communicating how much you don't like each other!"

If we didn't give priority to fostering our friendship, no matter how skilled we became at communicating, it just wouldn't serve us well. Although we wanted to continue improving on our communication, we wanted to be careful to work on our friendship even more.

CHAPTER FOUR

We Can't Flip a Coin for Everything

◆ DECISIONS ◆

My Husband's Obsession with Charts

The first major decision we made as a couple came shortly after our engagement. Tim had surprised me by proposing in Toronto over the Easter long weekend and a few weeks after that, I flew to Vancouver for a short visit. Aside from a friend's wedding we were to attend, we had a big order of business we hoped to complete while I was in town: We wanted to purchase our first apartment together. We had 12 days to find something we liked.

After our initial meeting with our real estate agent, we sat down to list out the qualities we were looking for in our first home together. Being the very thorough thinker that Tim was, he excitedly suggested, "Let's generate a chart based on these characteristics. We can rank each characteristic's importance from one to five. Then, for each property we look at, we can assign a numerical rating for each attribute and then calculate the final 'score' based on those ratings!" He quickly developed a spreadsheet with formulas that would automatically multiply and add up the score. Personally, I thought Tim was going a little overboard with the chart, but we were new at making big decisions together so since it seemed to make him feel more comfortable, I was happy to oblige.

Internal vs. Verbal Processing

Even while we were dating, we noticed a major difference in how we approached decision-making. I was an internal processor, while Tim was a verbal processor. This meant that I would observe a situation, mull it over in my head, weigh out the options in my heart, maybe journal a bit and be ready to announce my decision. Tim, on the other hand would gather the facts, discuss the options with his parents, siblings and other friends, talk it over with me, take a poll on Facebook, have more conversations with people, talk to me some more and "try on" the different outcomes before committing to one. I tended to rely more on intuition whereas Tim tended to rely more on reason.

Before we understood these differences about ourselves, we would drive each other crazy. Tim would be taken by surprise at my decisions because I hadn't consulted him about any of it. After all, he couldn't hear all the internal dialogue that had been going on in my head. He would feel left behind in the process. I, on the other hand, would think Tim was being wishy-washy. I couldn't understand how he could swing like a pendulum from one option today to another option tomorrow. I would think to myself, "Why can't he just decide already!" Tim needed more time to arrive at his conclusion – even though the end result was sometimes no different than mine.

The way we made decisions was partly due to how we were wired, but our families of origin also influenced us. I was an only child who grew up in an environment where I was given a lot of independence regarding my decisions, so I never really practiced including others in my decision-making process. Tim grew up with two siblings in a family that often consulted each other before decisions were made. When we got together, we had to learn the other partner's process so that we could understand their reasoning and allot sufficient time accordingly.

Forging Our Own Path

In our first year of marriage, we faced a lot of first-time decisions as a couple. While we loved and respected the families we came from, we also wanted to be intentional about making the decisions our own. Rather than blindly keeping with the traditions we grew up with, we wanted to make a new decision that was "ours."

We were now our own family and we, not our parents, would set the direction for ourselves. For example, in my childhood home, we always opened our Christmas presents on Boxing Day (which, if you're not from Canada, is the day after Christmas Day). That's the way my parents said it was done. Tim's family opened one gift each on Christmas Eve and the rest on the morning of Christmas Day – always together. The first Christmas after we got married, we had to decide for ourselves what our tradition would be. What we decided on was making crepes for brunch on Christmas Day and opening our gifts afterwards.

An Aside on Parent and In-Law Relationships

Tim and I were blessed to have come from homes where both sets of our parents had realistic expectations on marriage. They understood that once we were married, the boundaries would change and they would support us more from the sidelines, so to speak. After we got married, we also had to make a shift in how we prioritized our relationships. Our spouse would now come before our parents. This meant that in any situation where our parents' view was at odds with our spouse's view, we would take our spouse's side and stand by our mate - even if we didn't totally agree with him or her. It felt unnatural at first, but doing this was actually one way we strengthened our marriage relationship and gave it room to grow.

Looking back, something we wish we had done more in our early years of marriage was to help each other develop the in-law relationship. While it may not be true for everyone, for us, the in-law relationship required a lot of work and effort. I had lived my entire life with my parents so I knew how to interact with them and engage with them. Tim, however, was new to the picture. Just because Tim called my parents,

"Mom" and "Dad," it didn't mean he automatically knew how to relate to them. This was especially true because Tim was the first "son" they had, so it was a big learning curve for both parties.

Before we had a child, we lacked the foresight to see that encouraging our spouse to develop stronger relationships with our own parents would actually set up a better family environment when our parents became our children's grandparents. Getting to know Tim's parents better was another way I could have gotten to know Tim better, too.

My Silly Expensive Taste

A principle that helped us a lot in making decisions was that whoever was "in charge" of a certain domain would have the final say. The other person would trust their judgment. It took us a while to figure this out.

Near the beginning of our marriage, I wanted to buy a really nice non-stick pan that cost about $100. It was made of excellent quality material and I trusted the brand. It would make cooking that much easier and more enjoyable for me, I thought. When I approached Tim with the idea of buying that pan, he said, "Why can't you just get a $10 non-stick pan?" I scrunched up my nose at him. For a few weeks, it was a point of tension between us and we let the question sit.

One day, Tim said to me, "I've been thinking, you're the one who spends the most time cooking, so I'll let you make the decision on what cookware to get." I felt affirmed and supported in my role and although I was a little surprised at Tim's change of heart, I went ahead and made my purchase. Then, not wanting to damage my expensive pan, Tim went and got himself a $10 one in case he wanted to fry an egg. Over time, I realized that I'd use his $10 pan just about as much as I'd use my $100 one. Sadly, they're both scratched up about the same amount now. I feel silly about my insistence on buying the expensive pan but I'm grateful that Tim let me "own" my decision and that he gave me grace to make mistakes, even if it cost us a hundred dollars.

Our Final Rule about Decisions

In our marriage, we agreed that for major decisions: YES + NO = NO.

After getting married, Tim wanted to start having kids soon. He was excited to be a father and loved playing with children. In his mind, he thought having kids after a year of marriage was perfect timing. I, on the other hand, was quite nervous about having kids. I wasn't used to interacting with children. I also wasn't sure I was ready for the difficulty of pregnancy or for the amount of energy it would take to care for a baby. I wanted to wait longer.

As we talked about this topic, we started understanding each other's point of view. But we also needed to make a decision that we both agreed upon about this area of our life. In the end we settled on trying for kids after we came back from a pre-planned family trip to Europe, which was when we would be married for about two years.

When it came to smaller decisions, whoever felt stronger about the outcome or whoever it impacted more would have the final say.

CHAPTER FIVE

Hello Permanent Roommate

◆ DIFFERENCES ◆

The Blanket Hog vs. The Bed Hog

One of the big adjustments when we first got married was learning to share a space together. When we were dating, we didn't live with each other, so there were quirks, preferences and habits we didn't know about the other person. There were also quirks, preferences and habits we didn't know about ourselves, until there was someone to point it out to us. Learning to live harmoniously with each other involved figuring out what our differences were and how to address them.

For about two months after our wedding, I would wake up teetering on the edge of our queen-sized bed only to look over and find Tim sprawled out in the center. What I didn't realize was that I had all the sheets and he was left shivering in the middle of the night. I would call him a bed hog and he would claim that he was just trying to get under the blankets!

Learning to sleep together in the same bed was one of the first big lessons for us in living together. It took us a while, but eventually, we were able to adjust to each other and sleep in peace.

You Mean It Bothers You When I Do This?

In my growing up years, one of my "jobs" at home was to clear the dinner table after we were finished eating. I developed a system where I stacked all the plates and bowls from largest to smallest so that I could bring everything over to the sink in one go and soak it all in the sink before washing them. I was proud of my efficiency.

Shortly after we were married, as we cleaned up after dinner one night, Tim hesitantly said to me, "Can you please not put that plate on top of the other one?"

"Why?" I asked him.

"Because that plate's oily, and if you put the other one on top, it'll get all oily, too."

Hm. I had never thought it that way. I figured we'd be washing them all in a couple minutes anyway. Wasn't that what the dish soap was there for? We had a conversation about it and since it wouldn't hurt for me to do things differently, I agreed to try to change my habit. I say, "try," because we're four years in and I still forget sometimes.

Unrealistic Expectations

Going into marriage, I had the expectation that once a couple was married, they shared everything like soap, shampoo, and toothpaste. People always joked about how couples argued over how the toothpaste was squeezed. It's like that in movies. And my parents shared all that stuff. It wasn't until after we got married that I realized my expectations had not been realistic. A married couple did not have to share everything.

It became clear to me that we had to distinguish between differences in surface matters and differences in deeper matters. Toothpaste and shampoo were surface. We could change our personal preferences to suit the other person's, or, we would be fine to continue with our original choices. If you peeked into our bathroom these days, you'd notice we each have our shampoo and our own toothpaste. I guess a side benefit of this set up was that we didn't have to fight over how the toothpaste was squeezed!

Sometimes It's Hard to Change

I had a tendency for collecting things I thought I could use in the future. Perhaps it was partly due to a mentality of thriftiness, but I liked to collect all sorts of stuff – bags, take-out containers, boxes, elastic bands, ribbons, gift wrap, twisty-ties, coupons, random scraps of paper… The list went on. I had a really hard time throwing things away. In contrast, Tim's motto was "things are meant to be used." So if we weren't going to use them, we should get rid of them. Tim often tried to get me to de-clutter.

As I thought about my obsession to keep all this stuff "just in case," I realized it came from a fear of not having enough. They were, in a sense, a safety net for me. If I had extra buffer, I reasoned, I would feel safer.

I wanted to change, but it would not be easy. In order to do so, I had some deeper issues I had to work through. I needed time to re-frame my thinking. I needed practice in throwing things away. I needed help. Thankfully, Tim was pretty patient with me in helping me purge and asking me if we really needed to keep something. We also made it a practice to have a once-a-year clean out of everything so that we would not collect too much.

I'm a Girl, You're a Boy

Tim was the first guy I'd ever shared a living space with. Well, aside from my dad. I did not grow up with brothers or guy cousins. And I didn't really have guy friends until university. In sum, I was rather unfamiliar with their species. Part of the adjustment process for me was discovering how our approaches to life could be so very different simply because of one chromosome's variance.

One of my favourite ways to relax was (and still is) to paint my toenails. There was something therapeutic in making my feet look pretty. The first time I did this after we were married, Tim walked into the living room one afternoon and I suddenly heard some sputtering sounds coming from his corner.

I turned to look at him. "What?"

"How can you breathe in here? This stuff is noxious!" he wheezed, gasping for air.

Shrugging my shoulders I said, "It's only nail polish." I made a mental note to my future self to paint my nails when

Tim wasn't around to ruin my happy place with his gagging.

As for Tim and his favourite way to relax? He liked to watch high adrenaline movies and sports where people fought and crashed into each other. I don't think I'll ever get that.

Marriage Roles: I Cook, You Budget

One of the questions our pre-marital counselors had us answer was what kinds of expectations we had for our roles within marriage. Did we expect the wife to take care of the food, laundry and finances? Would the husband's role include looking after the car, the yard and fixing up the house?

To divvy up the responsibilities, we first looked at whether a certain area was one of our strengths or passions. Since Tim was infinitely better with numbers than I was, it seemed natural that he looked after our finances. Since I was more passionate about food, I would take care of the groceries and cooking. For things that neither of us was that great at or passionate about, we flipped a coin. Just kidding. Some tasks, like doing the dishes, we would share responsibility for. And others, like fixing stuff in the house, just wouldn't get done (until my dad would visit and then he'd receive from us a list of things to fix. Thanks, Dad!).

Why We Love Google Calendar

The other main logistical item for us to figure out involved time commitments. Who was going to be where and when was everything happening? Since I was in charge of cooking and Tim had a flexible work schedule, it became clear pretty early on in our marriage that I needed some way of tracking when he would be home for meals and when he needed me to pack him lunch. We began setting aside half an hour on Sunday evenings to touch base and go over the upcoming week with each other. He would have his calendar and I would have mine. Over time, we migrated to sharing our Google calendars with each other so we could always see what the other person's week looked like.

Calendar sharing and weekly check-ins were also invaluable to us when it came to figuring out our social engagements. Being the introvert that I am, I could only comfortably handle one to two social commitments per week. Tim, on the other hand, needed to see people quite a bit more than I did. So as we looked over our calendars, we would also assess which invitations we would accept together, which ones Tim would attend by himself, and which engagements we would decline.

Adjusting the Well-Oiled Machine

It felt great when there was a weekly rhythm in place and we knew each other well enough not to be bothered by our differences. But the reality was, we were constantly changing as people, and our circumstances were constantly changing as well. The initial adjustment required the most work, but to thrive as permanent roommates, we needed to be continually adjusting, evaluating, and adjusting some more. We were glad to have set a solid foundation with good habits early on, because when life became more complex and challenges arose (not to mention when Alena was born and everything changed completely), it was a relief to know that home was a place of safety and stability.

CHAPTER SIX

Waiting for the Sun to Rise

◆ HARDSHIP ◆

My Burnout Experience (Olive's story)

I was very ill and I didn't know it. Like a fog that had slowly rolled in, I gradually found myself feeling exhausted, indecisive, insecure and unwilling to engage with people. I was living overseas as an international student at the time and the thought of going to class brought an alarming sense of anxiety. I didn't want to leave the house, take the bus and interact with students and teachers. On the outside, I looked fine. On the inside, however, I was a mess.

A simple typing assignment alerted me that I was in trouble. As I transcribed an article on the symptoms, causes and remedies for burnout, I felt like I was writing about my own life. The symptoms I had chalked up to being effects of living in another country turned out to be telltale signs of burnout.

At my lowest point, I felt incapacitated. Unable to make simple decisions, I asked my roommate to pick up some groceries for me because being in a supermarket was too overwhelming. I slept both endlessly and restlessly. My stomach was constantly in knots and it took herculean effort to simply get dressed for the day. My sense of self-worth was shot, yet I became very self-absorbed. It was as if I had no room in my heart for other people because merely making it through each day consumed everything I had.

Looking back, it was 14 years of high-paced living that got me to that point. Realizing I needed help, I moved back to Canada and stayed under my parents' care for six months while meeting regularly with a counselor to sort through my mess. My counselor told me it would take at least 3 years to recover. He was right.

It was during my first year of recovery that Tim and I were engaged and got married. I felt bad for Tim that he was getting a broken wife and that my capacity was so limited. I also felt terribly fragile. The foundations of my life had been demolished and I faced the daunting task of rebuilding. My consolation was that I did not have to rebuild alone.

How My Husband Helped Me Most

Living with my burned-out self was annoying at times. I was

constantly battling my limitations and comparing my present self to my former energetic self. I felt ridiculously needy. In those moments, Tim would listen to my frustrations and fears and affirm his love for me. He would remind me of the baby steps of progress I had already made and reignite my sense of hope that one day this dark night would pass.

I remember on certain days when I felt especially weak, I would look at Tim and ask him to please pray for me. He would sit down, take my hands in his and pray. And then he would give me a hug – a physical reminder that I was accepted and cherished, even in my broken state.

Another huge way Tim helped me in my recovery process was by agreeing to have me work part-time when I finally felt able to work again. He understood that post-burnout, my economy was no longer based on time, but on energy. The limiting factor in my day was how much capacity I had in me, not how much time I had on my hands. That meant that there would be slots in our calendar that would look blank, but I would actually be doing the work of resting.

Tim encouraged me toward health and wholeness in whichever ways I felt would help me most. That included time for solitude, but also time with select people. He supported me in seeing a counselor, finding a spiritual director, spending time with close friends and, for two years, enrolling in a Spiritual Formation program through a local Bible college.

Most of all, Tim believed in the person I was becoming.

The Challenge of Having a Burnt Out Wife

When I was thinking about proposing to Olive, one of my biggest worries was that I wouldn't have the strength to love her. She was recovering from burnout and it would be a long process. How much help would she need along the way? Would I be able to care for her well? What if she never recovered fully?

There were inconveniences of having a wife with low energy. During her recovery she needed a lot of rest and tired easily. Our activities were restricted by how she felt. This was not how I imagined marriage to be. I wanted us to go out and have fun together – to travel, host parties, go snowboarding, visit friends, and enjoy life to the fullest. I was disappointed when we had to turn down invitations from friends.

Other times I went to functions alone. "Where's Olive?" people would always seem to ask me. I never really knew how to respond. Not wanting to give the same response, I rotated explanations: She's tired. She's not feeling well. She has schoolwork to do. With closer friends, I would venture to provide an explanation closer to the truth, but I always wondered if they really understood. I worried about how others would perceive my new wife and did not want them to think of her as fragile and weak.

Looking Out for Her Best Interest

When Olive burnt out, I started educating myself on this illness. I did some of my own research and reading, and I spent time listening to Olive and trying to understand what she was feeling.

With the decision to marry Olive came the commitment to journey with her through burnout recovery, no matter how long it took and where it would lead. I had to accept the fact that the woman I married might never return back to her "normal" self and make the choice to love her no matter how burnout impacted her.

Part of me was embarrassed at Olive's lack of energy. Living in a culture that idolized success and accomplishments, I had believed that a person's worth was closely tied to her productivity. This embarrassment caused me to be impatient with Olive's seeming lack of progress. It was difficult to accept the slowness of the process. But I knew she didn't have control over this.

Part of me was proud of Olive's courage and strength in facing the hardships of burnout recovery. It was certainly a challenge to live life having her energy cut in half. Deep down, there was a voice that reminded me that Olive's value did not depend on what she was able to accomplish.

In the midst of the tension of embarrassment and pride, I started to understand what love was. Love was without condition. As Olive journeyed through burnout recovery, I had to make the repeated choice to recognize Olive's worth and value apart from what she could or could not do. My job was to believe in her when she didn't believe in herself.

A practical way I helped was by protecting her limited supply of energy. A few summers ago, we took a trip to Europe with my family. I knew I needed to make sure our itinerary would not be too demanding on Olive. Usually when I travelled, I tried to fit in as much as I could into one day. Travelling with my wife was different. On our first day in Paris our family had planned to tour several hot spots in the city. In the afternoon, we left our family and returned to the hotel so Olive could nap. Though I missed out on seeing part of the city, I made it my priority to have Olive rest so she could enjoy the remainder of the day.

Some days Olive would try to do too much - it was difficult for her to accept her limits. I reminded her to take breaks and be kind to herself. I learned to notice signs of Olive's tiredness and prompt her to rest.

Over time, Olive has found a new "normal." Her capacity for work is smaller than her pre-burnout days and her need for rest is greater. However, both of us have slowly learned to accept and embrace the changes.

Facing Depression (Tim's story)

Depression has been a familiar and unwelcome companion in the last decade of my life. His visits are always unannounced and extremely difficult. Depression has felt more like an intruder than a guest. When he is with me, I am lethargic, unmotivated, weary, and sad. Most days I feel frustrated at myself. Other days I wish I could die. I am always relieved when Depression leaves me.

One of my biggest fears in getting married was what would happen if I became depressed. What would my wife think? How would she respond? What would I do?

My fears came true.

Depression came for several visits during our first three years of marriage. The shortest stay was two months. The longest was half a year. These excerpts from my journal show how I felt during these times:

"Yesterday morning I was so emotionally tired – I just started sleeping from my exhaustion. I feel like giving up… it is too difficult to have all these questions and doubts. I'm tired of my disbelief."

"I feel down and sad. Life feels so heavy now. Everything I

do feels so difficult – I need to force myself to do them: my work, exercise, socializing, and especially waking up. I really dislike having to force myself to do things – it is very tiring."

The first time I became depressed while married, I discovered that it would be impossible to hide it from my wife. It was difficult to pretend to be strong when I felt the exact opposite. Acting like I was okay felt like living a lie; I felt like a fraud. So I tried to be honest with Olive. It was hard to express how I felt and what I was going through. It was like showing her the dark side of myself – the part of me that I was disgusted at and embarrassed about.

Many times I felt guilty for being depressed, and especially guilty for being a depressed husband to Olive. I felt like a sinking ship and I constantly worried that I was taking my wife down with me – that she was trapped and had no where to go. I feared I would lose my job because I had no energy to work, and then Olive would have to be the primary breadwinner. I worried that if we had kids and I got depressed, she would essentially be a single parent who would also have the additional burden of a depressed husband to take care of.

Though it was comforting to have someone to confide in, every time I talked with Olive I felt like a broken record, retelling the same pitiful story of my crappy life over and over again. I felt sorry for Olive, having to listen to my depressive thoughts every day.

Wait with Me

It made a world of a difference having my wife walk with me through depression. In the past, while I was going through depression, I came across many people who tried to help. Most would give me advice and suggestions of what I could do to "get better" or "feel better." Sometimes I appreciated their concern, but most of the time I would only become more frustrated because I had tried everything they had suggested. It made me feel like all they wanted to do was "fix" me. Looking back, I've come to the realization that although many people want to help, most do not know how. Luci Shaw in her book *God in the Dark* said, "The classic misinterpretation of the healthy on the sick is that wellness is a matter of choice and decision."[3]

With Olive, things were different. As I showed Olive my depression, she responded by trying to understand how I felt and affirming that she still loved me. Each time I shared, her response would dispel a bit of the fear that I had that she would leave me or stop loving me because of my depression. With each response, I gained courage to be more vulnerable and honest with her.

Having someone to share with gave me courage to acknowledge what I was feeling. Rather than try to come up with an easy solution or a list of things to try, Olive promised to journey with me as I figured things out. In the midst of this, she communicated to me that her love for me was not conditional of the things I could do, or being the best I could be – but that she loved me regardless of those things. Though I knew this in my head, going through depression and experiencing Olive's love for me helped convince my heart of this truth.

As Olive walked with me, I stopped hiding from my depression and started facing it. With the encouragement of my wife, I started talking to a counselor about my depression for the first time. The counseling sessions helped me become aware of what was going on and uncover the causes.

Olive gave me the space I needed. She didn't always ask me how I was doing, though I knew she wanted to know. I didn't feel suffocated by her. This was a relief as it was hard to articulate what was going on and frustrating trying to express my feelings.

But always, in small and big ways, my wife showed me that she cared for me and loved me. Some days she would buy my favourite chocolate bar and wrap it up to give to me. On my 29th birthday, in the midst of my depression, she surprised me with tickets to see my favourite hockey team.

Dr. Sharon Smith, an expert in mental health, said the best thing to do to help someone going through depression is to wait with him or her. It is like sitting beside them in the dark, waiting for the sun to rise.[4] That was what Olive did for me. She waited patiently with me for months and months for the light to come.

Limping Along with My Husband

The first time Tim allowed me to see his depression I was slightly shocked. I had come into the marriage thinking I was the one who needed mending. I hadn't realized that Tim also walked with a limp. It dawned on me that we would need to hobble along together for a while.

Living with a sick person is challenging. Living with a person whose illness not visible is even more challenging. Having experienced burnout with its symptoms that were similar to depression, I could identify the red flags when they presented themselves. I also had a sense of what might be helpful to Tim and what was not. Yet, watching him suffer and struggle through it day to day was painful.

It was frustrating too, because I often felt just as tired, but I didn't have the option of curling up in bed and sleeping the day away. One of us had to keep things going, right?

One of the big challenges of living with a depressed person was dealing with my own impatience. "When will this end?" was frequently on my heart. I wanted to "fix" his problems, to ask the right question that might illuminate his soul and draw him out of the slump, to solve the mystery of what it was that weighed him down so that he could live lightly and freely again. I wanted my happy husband back. I had to continually remind myself that time was the main ingredient for healing and that the most helpful thing I could do was simply accompany Tim in the process.

Seeing Beyond the Darkness

Each time the depression came, I faced certain fears: Tim wanted extra time to rest and reflect, but was I coddling him and making matters worse by letting him sleep and spend hours on the couch? On the flip side, was I asking too much of him if I expected him to do the dishes, for example? If I picked up the slack around the house, would he feel like I was trampling over his sense of dignity?

There was also the matter of wanting to know what was going on in his mind and heart yet also giving him space. I felt uncertain about how much he wanted to talk. I learned to be gentle in broaching the topic and open-handed in how long each conversation might last.

In seasons of depression, I learned that an important thing

I could do was to encourage Tim to pay attention to what was going on inside of him. I believed that there was deep work being done during those times and my ability to help Tim was very limited. I suggested that he find a counselor and take a mini-retreat. One time, I wrote up encouraging words on sticky notes and posted them around the house in the middle of the night. When he awoke the next morning, he was surprised to see the various reminders of his worth and God's promises. I also prayed for him.

Waiting in the darkness with Tim pushed me to look beyond myself for strength. It was especially in those times that I would turn to God for patience, grace and reassurance of love – things that we both needed but did not possess enough of on our own.

Through it all, I chose to believe that depression did not define the man I married. It was challenging and it was a life-shaping experience, but these times were merely stops along the road of fully becoming the person he was made to be.

CHAPTER SEVEN

Naked and Unashamed

◆ LOVE ◆

The "N" Word

Before we were married, I couldn't even say the word "naked" without blushing. I remember sitting in the car after our premarital counseling session – the one where we talked about our expectations for sex – looking at Tim, and squeaking out something like "negid" in between my giggles. Maybe I was more immature than most people, but the idea of wearing nothing in front of someone other than my reflection in a mirror was hard for me to wrap my head around. Could I ever become that comfortable with this man? I wondered.

As it turned out, getting physically naked was not the hardest part. Uncovering and exposing my true self – and then allowing what I'd exposed to be loved – was the real challenge.

The irony was that as much as I wanted to be deeply known, it was also terrifying. Showing off the good stuff was not the problem. The difficulty lay in exposing the not-so-good stuff; the stuff I didn't like about myself; the stuff I'd rather hide. What I found beautiful about marriage was that two people could allow themselves to be seen (in all senses) without feeling ashamed.

As Tim and I thought about what our wedding vows would mean to us, we envisioned our marriage to be a safe place where we could continue discovering and revealing who we were to the other person. It would take time to build that trust, and we knew we could only do it in the context of a commitment to love each other without condition.

You're Not the Same Person I Married!

"The wife you kiss goodbye in the morning is the not the same wife you come home to in the evening. The husband who walks out the door in the morning is not the same husband who greets you at night." When our premarital counselors told us this before we were married, I was shocked. What did they mean my husband comes home a different person?! What they were saying was this: Over the course of a day, what he had seen, heard and thought would transform who he was.

This was an exciting thought. Our marriage was a dynamic relationship! There would always be something new to learn about my husband. The changes could be small, so small that it might seem trivial to talk about some of them. But give it a year, or a decade, and all of the sudden, if I didn't keep paying attention to how he had changed, I might wake up and wonder who I was sharing my bed with.

"What did you read today?" was a question I asked Tim during one of his times of depression. He shared with me that he came across the idea that depression was not an enemy, but rather a friend. It was a shift in his view of the world that had implications on how he would face his illness. Had I not prompted the conversation and had he not been open with me, I would never have known.

Continuing to grow in my knowledge of my husband allows my love for him to keep expanding as well. The more I know about him, the more of him my love encompasses. It also enables me to love who he really is in the present moment and safeguards me against loving merely my impression of him.

A Daily Connection Point

In our first year of marriage, I was especially keen on establishing a rhythm of having a time of daily connection. Being people with a faith background, we would pray together every day. Sometimes before we'd pray, we'd ask each other: What gave you life today? What took life away from you today? Or alternatively, what are you grateful for or worried about today?

We found that it worked best for us to do this at night, just before we went to sleep. Sometimes, if I wanted to sleep earlier than Tim did, I would ask him to come pray with me first. If Tim happened to be out and I was heading to bed, we would pray over the phone. They weren't necessarily long prayers. Sometimes, we would simply say, "Thanks for loving us, God!" Other nights, if one of us was feeling particularly wiped, we'd just let the other person pray on behalf of both of us. Most nights, we let our prayers be a way to review the day and to bring our cares to God. It took a while for the habit to get established, but it has become one of our most cherished times of the day.

The Fun Factor

Before we were married, I never played computer games. I thought they were a waste of my time. Then Tim came along and introduced me to this very simple, but highly addictive game called Bejeweled Blitz. It didn't take me long to discover that matching coloured gems within the pressure of sixty seconds was actually very fun. Especially when I could get a high score that would beat Tim's high score!

We recognized that if we were not having fun and laughing, we were setting ourselves up for trouble. The ability to have fun together meant that we enjoyed each other's company. We wanted to remain best friends, because why would we want to spend the rest of our lives with someone we didn't like hanging around?

Our little game of Bejeweled became one of the ways for us to remember to have fun in the midst of life's stress and challenges. A weekly date night was another. To keep growing our love, we needed times of being serious as well as being silly.

Taking It Into the Bedroom

My brother-in-law was the only person who gave us a book about sex for our wedding. It had a bright orange cover and was titled, *The Idiot's Guide to Amazing Sex*. I think he sensed that we had no clue what we were doing; that we were indeed idiots when it came to sex. We had a lot to learn. But what he may not have realized is the importance of his gift to us. Establishing a great sex life was a key part of setting a good foundation for our marriage.

Starting out was awkward. It was not as spontaneous or intuitive as the movies had led us to believe. It didn't even feel great at first. But over time, we learned. We became students of each other and to help us continue learning, we read books, experimented and yes, we even put it into our schedules.

It's been said that if you want to gauge the health of a marriage, look at the couple's sex life. If the relationship is drifting or strained, one of the first things to go is sex. On the flip side, we have learned that regular naked time is one of the surefire ways to strengthen our bond as husband and wife.

When I Don't Feel the Love

In the months after we got married, we were in the "honeymoon" phase. Marriage was new and exciting, and most days we were just delighted to be married. In the mornings I would wake up, look over at my husband and wonder if I was dreaming. We really were married! Those days it was easy to show love to him.

As the months went by, the newness of the marriage subsided. The intense feelings of love we initially felt also subsided. I started encountering the challenge and difficulty of loving my husband when I wasn't feeling it.

The hardest times were after both of us had a long day, both of us were dead tired, and something needed to get done. Dinner needed to be cooked, the garbage taken out, or the dishes washed. And neither of us felt like it. The choice to show love to Tim during those times was extremely difficult, because it required sacrifice.

Author Tim Keller wrote in his book, *The Meaning of Marriage,*

"In any relationship, there will be frightening spells in which your feelings of love seem to dry up. And when that happens you must remember that the essence of a marriage is that it is a covenant, a commitment, a promise of future love. So what do you do? You do the acts of love, despite your lack of feeling. You may not feel tender, sympathetic, and eager to please, but in your actions you must be tender, understanding, forgiving, and helpful. And, if you do that, as time goes on you will not only get through the dry spells, but they will become less frequent and deep, and you will become more constant in your feelings. This is what can happen if you decide to love."[5]

When I was single, I idealized being in love and getting married. It would feel so good and I would be so happy. Love seemed so great. Everything in life would seem easier when I was with someone I loved. Or so I thought.

After getting married I realized that love was difficult. It was inconvenient. It was hard. It was a lot of work. It was sacrifice. All of a sudden, love didn't seem as appealing anymore. The reality was that a love that was shown only when I felt "in love" was merely a shallow love. Love that was shown in the midst of a lack of feelings was more difficult, but also a deeper, truer love.

Love that Lasts a Lifetime

Everyone seems to remind everyone else that one in two marriages will end in divorce. I'm not sure why people like to focus on this fact. Why not talk about how one in two marriages last for a lifetime? I think it is an incredible yet extremely challenging feat that two people would stay married for a lifetime.

Our hope and intention is for our marriage to last a lifetime. Recently, Tim and I celebrated 4 years of marriage. If we live until we are 77 years old and remain married, then we will be married for 50 years. This means that Tim and I have only experienced 8% of our married life. That's not very long.

We hope that this is just the beginning of a long journey together, God-willing.

Being in a marriage is like building a cathedral. Each day my husband and I lay a few more bricks. And the next day, we lay a few more bricks on top of what we have already built. Knowing that Tim and I intend to build our marriage for a lifetime gives me meaning and hope. Meaning because I know that the work I put into my marriage will be the foundation on which our future will be built – it reminds me to be careful and deliberate in how I build. It gives me hope because I know that down the road, we will be able to admire what we have built together over time, and to reap the rewards of our efforts.

Author Dietrich Bonhoeffer, when he was in prison in

Germany during World War II, wrote this to his sister for her wedding day, "It is not your love that sustains the marriage, but from now on, the marriage that sustains your love."[6] My desire is that together with Tim, we can build and experience a love that has been sustained by marriage over the course of a lifetime.

Epilogue

A month before we got married, Olive and I set up a TV on the balcony of our new apartment. Sitting on an old futon and covered in a blanket, we watched the movie *Stardust*[7] in our very own exclusive outdoor summer theatre.

In the movie, Yvaine (played by Claire Danes) is a star from the sky that has been injured and falls to the earth. Because of her injury, she loses her shine, and is mistaken as a normal human being by the main character, Tristan (played by Charlie Cox). Their relationship starts off rocky but over the course of their adventure together, they grow a fondness for each other.

One particular scene from the movie stays in my mind and paints a beautiful picture of marriage for me: In the middle of their adventure, they are guests on a flying pirate ship. The ship's captain is teaching Yvaine how to dance. As they are dancing, Tristan taps the captain's shoulder and cuts in to dance with Yvaine. At first they start dancing together shyly. But as the dancing continues, Yvaine starts experiencing the love Tristan has for her. As the scene pans out, you watch their delight. And then you notice it – Yvaine begins to light up. Her shine is returning to her.

What I look forward to with much anticipation is to help Olive shine. I believe that as Olive experiences my growing love for her, the love of her friends and family, and God's profound love towards her, she will continue growing and blossoming as a person. I have started to see this happen. One of the deepest joys in my four years of marriage has been to watch my wife grow in beauty.

My hope in marriage is to be an integral part of my wife becoming her true, authentic self. I am excited to have a lifelong front-row seat to witness her shine brighter and become a beautiful gift to the world.

The morning I walked down the aisle as a bride, one phrase kept repeating itself in my head: *Today, I am marrying my favourite stranger.* Excitement and fear mingled together in my heart. I'd managed to get five hours of sleep the night before, but my body betrayed my nervousness when I threw up my vitamins. Somehow, I didn't dare speak my thought to anyone though. I was committing to love this man for the rest of my life, shouldn't he be more than a stranger to me by now? Well, he was. And he wasn't. Four years later, he still is my favourite stranger. He's just a little more familiar now.

When I think about our future together, I hope and pray that Tim would always remain just that: my absolute favourite and most familiar stranger.

Appendix: *Our Conversation Guide for Blue Day*

During our Blue Days, these are the ten topics we would discuss and the questions we would ask ourselves.

1) The Big Picture

This includes our life goals as individuals and as a couple. What do we feel called to do in our lives? Is there anything new we have discovered about ourselves? What are our 5, 10 or 20-year dreams and goals? Also included are our personal mission statements as well as our mission statement as a couple and family. We also use this time to review our wedding vows to remind us of what we want our marriage to be about.

2) Marriage

This block of time is used to assess where our relationship is at as husband and wife. How is our marriage doing? Is there any unresolved conflict we need to talk about? How are our date nights? Is there anything we want to change or improve? How is our sex life? What are we going to do to continue building our relationship? (e.g., Is there a book we want to read or a marriage conference to attend? Etc.)

3) Family

This includes our relationships with immediate family (our

parents, siblings and eventually, children). It also includes relationships with extended family. How can we be intentional about developing these relationships? Since both sets of our parents live in other cities, we also look at when we are able to see them in person and whether we're happy with the current frequency of communication with them. Other questions include: When do we hope to have children? How many children do we want?

4) Friends

For this category, we divide it into people who are friends to both of us, as well as individual close friendships for each of us. We want to be intentional about spending time with people who can encourage us to keep growing. We ask ourselves: Who are our current close friends? Who do we want to spend more time with? When do we want to see them? Who would we rather spend less time with?

5) Faith Community

Here we address our involvement in a faith community. Initially, we were simply looking for a church to attend. Eventually, we started volunteering to lead a group. Our church also offered several service times, so we discussed which service we wanted to regularly participate in. Questions to ask include: How do we want to serve at this church? Which relationships do we want to develop here and how do we want to invest in them? Do we want to change the way(s) we are involved (e.g., join the choir, take a course, or cut back on something else)?

6) Work

Here we talk about our careers. Are we living out what we believe we are made for and called to do? Are there any major conferences, deadlines, etc. that the other person needs to be aware of? Are we satisfied with how many hours of work we are putting in per week? What are our next steps for developing our careers (training, education, new job, etc.)?

7) Rest

This area includes our weekly day of rest, leisure activities and vacation. Questions include: Are we getting enough rest? What do we want to do for vacation this year? How do we want to spend our vacation days? Where do we want to travel to and with whom? Are we being consistent about keeping one day a week that is purely about recharging and enjoying God, each other and life? Are there any significant milestones we want to celebrate and how shall we celebrate them (e.g., Tim's 30th birthday)? Are there new fun activities we want to try?

8) Growth and Health

This includes all spheres of health: physical, emotional, spiritual and mental. How have we been feeling? Are there certain checkups we need to make appointments for? Do we have a place to keep track of our health? Any exercise goals? Do either of us feel a need to see a counselor? What books do we want to read to help us grow? What is currently working well for us (e.g., Olive wants to continue meeting with a

Spiritual Director every month) and what needs changing?

9) Life Infrastructure

Anything related to our home or car goes here. Questions include: Is there anything that needs fixing (e.g., the window seals are broken)? Is there anything that needs to be thrown away (e.g., old laptops)? Do we need to make any purchases (e.g., a new lamp for the living room)? Are we hoping to move to a bigger home? If so, when? How is the condition of our car?

10) Finances

Usually, we look at this topic last because our finances support everything else that we do. We want to spend our money on the things that we value in life so establishing a budget is part of this. In the first year of marriage, we needed to merge bank accounts and set up credit cards with both our names. Questions to look at here include: Is our budget realistic and is there anything we need to adjust? Are there areas we are spending more/less than budgeted? What organizations or charities do we want to give to and how much? Are we saving enough money? Are there any large purchases we need to discuss? Are we living within our means and being the best stewards of the finances we have been given?

Notes

1. Parrott, Drs. Les and Leslie, *I Love You More: How Everyday Problems Can Strengthen Your Marriage*. (Grand Rapids: Zondervan, 2005), 122-123.

2. For more information on the Birkman Method® Personality Test, go to www.birkman.com

3. Shaw, Luci, *God in the Dark*. (East Sussex: Highland Books, 1990), 160.

4. Smith, Dr. Sharon, Lecture. Tenth Church. Vancouver, BC, Canada. 23 Jan, 2011.

5. Keller, Dr. Timothy, *The Meaning of Marriage: Facing the Complexities of Commitment with the Wisdom of God*. (New York: Dutton, 2011), 96.

6. Bonhoeffer, Dietrich. *Letters & Papers From Prison*. (New York: Touchstone, 1997).

7. Bonaventura, L., Dreyer, M., Gaiman, N., & Vaughn, M. (Producers), & Vaughn, M. (Director). (2007). *Stardust* [Motion picture]. United States: Paramount Pictures.

About the Authors

When no one's around to hear them at home, Tim and Olive's life turns into a musical. Some of their best memories together include eating at a seaside McDonald's in Casablanca, riding bikes around Barcelona, having pasta in Panama to celebrate their first Valentine's Day together, and  making banana-nutella crepes for brunch.

Tim is a cheerful pessimist born in Yellowknife. He holds a business degree and has worked in logistics and non-profit. He loves mangos, snowboarding, mentoring, the Vancouver Canucks, analyzing everything, and laughing with his daughter. His favourite person is his wife. Tim works as a social media, marketing, and blogging consultant.

Olive is an artsy optimist who grew up in Toronto. Her favourite place in the world is her home. A contemplative at heart, she aspires to be a conduit of grace, rest and beauty in this hurried and chaotic world.

Tim and Olive were married in the autumn of 2008 and live with their daughter Alena near Vancouver, Canada. They regularly blog about thoughtful marriage, parenting, and life at www.timandolive.com.

Also by these Authors:

Thoughtful and laugh-out-loud funny, *Then Came The Baby: The Wonder, Mayhem, and Hilarity of our First Year as Parents* is one couple's candid, entertaining and reflective answer to the question, "What's it like to be a first-time parent?"

With the same engaging storytelling as their first book (*Fight With Me*), Tim

and Olive recount the joys, challenges, poignant moments and lessons learned from pregnancy to their daughter's first birthday. Written in a personal "he said/she said" style, they offer an uncensored view of the remarkable roller coaster experience that is first-time parenthood, inviting the reader along for the ride. *Then Came the Baby* is available for purchase at Amazon.

"Tim and Olive open the windows of their home and life together as a married couple and new parents, baring their souls in an honest and winsome way."

- Mike Woodard, author of Love That Lasts

"Refreshing and encouraging, fun (and funny), reassuring and very honest."

- Jess Versteeg, blogger at Bucket List Journey

Made in the USA
San Bernardino, CA
07 June 2017